Copyright © 2022 by Family Tree Publishing

All rights reserved. No part of this book may be reproduced or used in any manner without written permission of the copyright owner except for the use of quotations in a book review.
For more information,
address: info@familytree.pub

Author Pamela Robbins
Book design by Eduardo Paj

ISBN: 978-1-957308-01-2
https://familytree.pub

Library of Congress Control Number: 2021925151

For Vivian~
All the best...
Dr. Pam
2023

BILLY
THE BUFFALO AND HIS BRIDE BARBARA

by Pamela Robbins
Illustrated by Eduardo Paj

This book is dedicated to my children and grandchildren.
May the love of learning and nature
be ever present and preserved.

Billy the Buffalo and his Bride Barbara
spend their days grazing and gazing,
and romping and rolling,
in the wide-open spaces they call home.

This is where they love to roam.

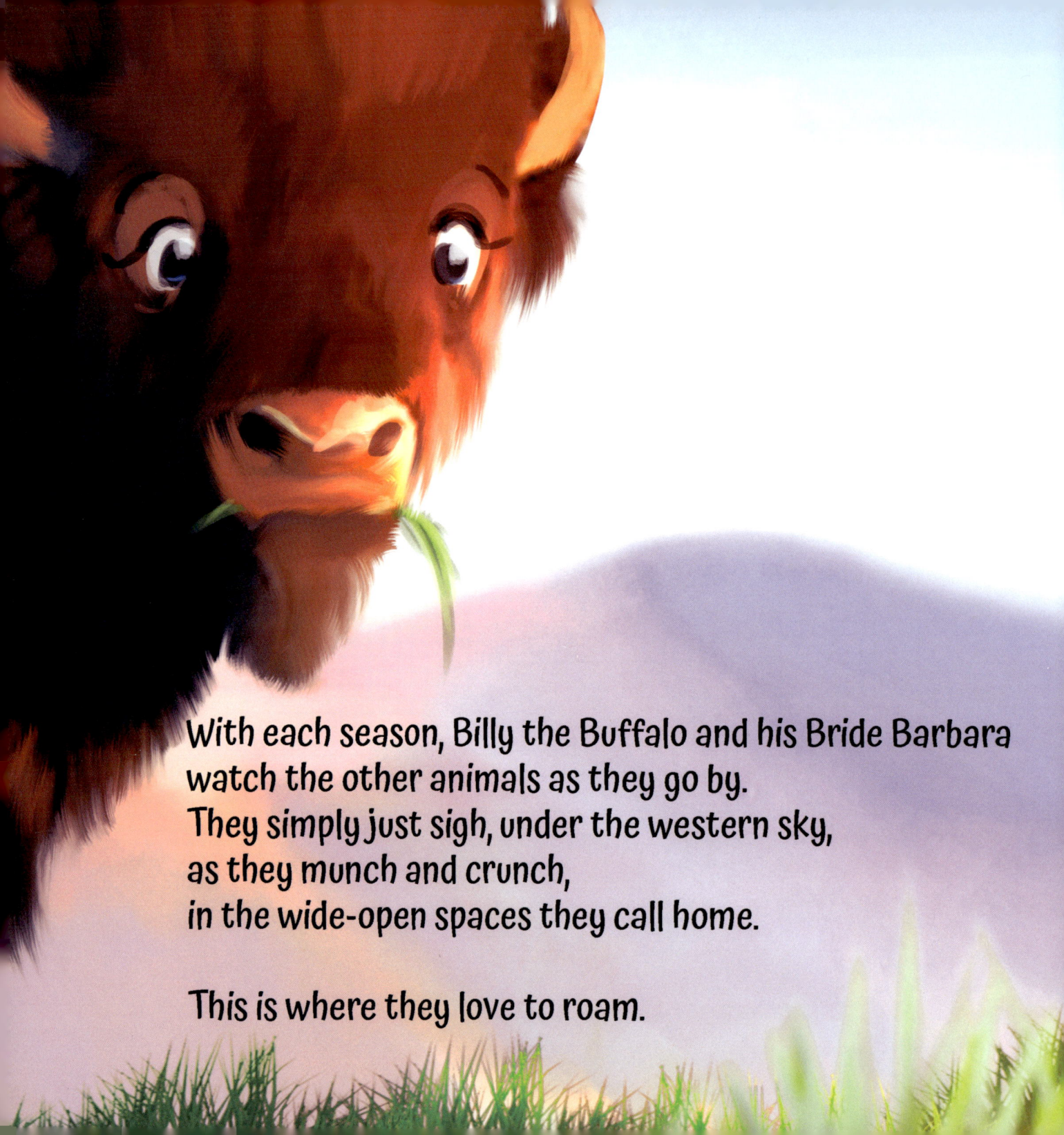

With each season, Billy the Buffalo and his Bride Barbara watch the other animals as they go by.
They simply just sigh, under the western sky,
as they munch and crunch,
in the wide-open spaces they call home.

This is where they love to roam.

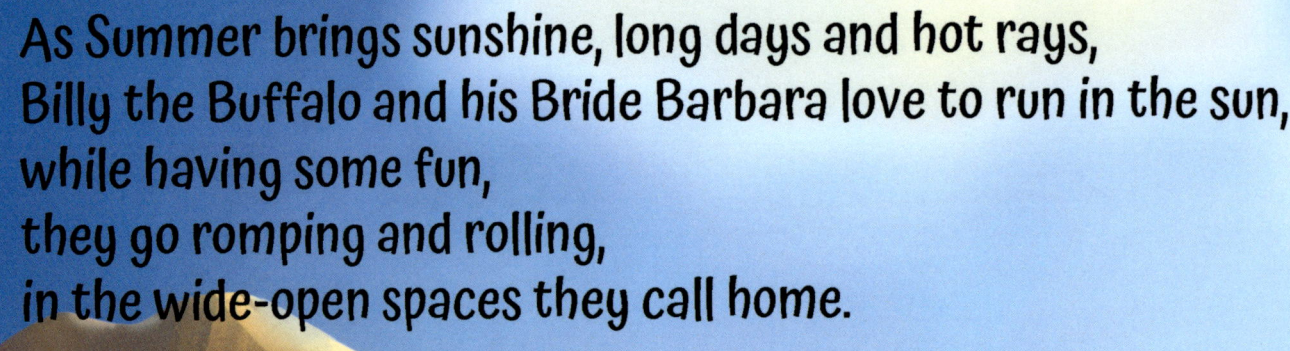

As Summer brings sunshine, long days and hot rays,
Billy the Buffalo and his Bride Barbara love to run in the sun,
while having some fun,
they go romping and rolling,
in the wide-open spaces they call home.

This is where they love to roam.

When Fall weather cools down,
they grow fluffy fur all around,
growing long towards the ground.
As they keep grazing and gazing, romping and rolling,
in the wide-open spaces they call home.

This is where they love to roam.

Soon, Winter air chills, and without making a sound,
snow covers the ground,
and Billy the Buffalo and his Bride Barbara dance all around.
While they go grazing and gazing, romping and rolling,
in the wide-open spaces they call home.

This is where they love to roam.

Spring brings new life abound;
as Billy the Buffalo and his Bride Barbara welcome
Baby Betty Buffalo here to follow around.
Soon, she begins, grazing and gazing, romping and rolling,
as she dances and prances,
in the wide-open spaces they call home.

This is where they love to roam.

Billy the Buffalo and his Bride Barbara,
pay no attention to the lizards that leap
or the snakes that slither beneath their feet.
As they go grazing and gazing, romping and rolling,
in the wide-open spaces they call home.

This is where they love to roam.

As the seasons go by,
they stare at the sky with wide open eyes.
They wander the west,
in search of the best,
as they go grazing and gazing, romping and rolling,
in the wide-open spaces they call home.

This is where they love to roam.

Once the wind starts to sigh, the clouds roll by,
and the birds fly high.
Billy the Buffalo and his Bride Barbara seem to know
the seasons are changing,
and it's time for rearranging,
in the wide-open spaces they call home.

This is where they love to roam.

Suddenly, the rain starts to pour,
and funny enough,
with a big giant huff,
they all start to snore.

They are at home in the wide-open spaces.
For this is where they love to roam.